A BEGINNER'S GUIDE TO
WORKING
TRIALS

WENDY BEASLEY

Dedication

To Rose Jones and Angus
(WT Ch Spinbrook Legionaire, CDex, UDex, WDex, PDex)
who introduced me to Working Trials,
and to Mike Snow with his wonderful Waggerland Collies
who offered help, advice and inspiration along the way.

t.f.h.

KINGDOM

contents

Acknowledgements

I would like to thank
Chris Farrer with Reuter and Carolyn Andrews with Jack and Harley
for all their help with the photographs
and my husband Paul
for his patience in taking them.

Also by the same author : **A Beginners Guide To Competitive Obedience**

To the uninitiated, Working Trials must seem a very peculiar pastime. Handlers and dogs gather at unearthly times, in outlandish places and often inclement weather. They then spend the day (or several days) jumping in and out of their cars and driving round the countryside in various directions, looking for judges standing in distant fields or sets of jumps on the horizon. For those who are used to competing at obedience shows with cut grass rings, level ground and adequate toilet facilities the Working Trials world comes as a bit of a shock – and I speak from personal experience. However, it is a sport that has a way of growing on you, and each small success spurs you on to greater effort.

Working Trials consists of groups of tests at different levels of competition referred to as *stakes* (not classes). Unlike in other dog events, competitors in Working Trials do not lose marks – they gain them. Marks are awarded out of a possible total for each test and, at the end of the stake, the marks are added up. The ultimate aim is to gain enough marks in each group of tests to qualify for the stake overall.

There are five stakes altogether: Companion Dog (CD), Utility Dog (UD), Working Dog (WD), Tracking Dog (TD) and Patrol Dog (PD). Each of these stakes is at two levels: Open and Championship. TD and PD are the two top stakes and are at the same level, each providing a route to Working Trial Champion status. To compete at the top level it is necessary to gain qualifications through the stakes, qualifying in both Open and Championship UD as well as gaining one Open and two Championship qualifications in WD. Dogs who have reached this stage may enter TD, PD or both at Open level. If they are awarded two Certificates of Merit (CoMs) at this level they are eligible to enter the Championship stake and compete for Working Trial Certificates (usually referred to as *tickets* by competitors). Winning a ticket qualifies a dog for competition in the annual Kennel Club Working Trial Championships, and two tickets in either stake or a combination of both under two different judges result in the title of Working Trials Champion.

Certificates of Merit are awarded at Open trials and, with the exception of the CD stake, it is necessary to gain a CoM (or two in the case of TD and PD) before entry into the equivalent stake at a Championship trial. CoMs are awarded at Open trials to dogs gaining no less than 80% of the overall marks for the stake and at least the minimum qualification mark in each individual group. Qualification at Championship level is achieved by gaining not less than 70% of the marks and results in the letters of the stake (for example, CD or UD) being added after the dog's name. However, if 80% of the overall total with at least the minimum in each section is gained, the dog will qualify for the stake Excellent and be entitled to these letters plus EX (for example, CDEX or UDEX). Qualifications must be Excellent to allow the dog to progress through the stakes.

Although there is a winner and second, third and fourth places at the end of each stake, in trials this is very much secondary to the qualification; until the top stakes, qualifying, not winning, is the way forward. The result is a very friendly atmosphere with competitors genuinely wishing each other well and pleased with other people's qualifications. The test is against a standard, not each other, so it is more a case of personal achievement than a need to win.

Working Trials are not so well known as some other canine activities and can be quite difficult to find out about. When I was involved in obedience competitions I was not alone in thinking of Working Trials as the poor relation, for dogs and handlers who could not make it in the obedience world. Sadly, this opinion is still widely held, and it was only by competing myself that I learned just how wrong it is. Trials and trials training are a great deal of fun for both handlers and dogs, but they are also extremely hard work, demanding immense dedication, determination and commitment to reach even a reasonable standard. They are not for the faint-hearted dog or handler, but are tremendously rewarding and as near as the ordinary person gets to 'real' Working conditions.

All Working Trials in the United Kingdom are governed by The Kennel Club (KC), although in Scotland some authority is delegated to the Scottish Kennel Club. The Irish Kennel Club governs events in Southern Ireland but the awards under Irish Kennel Club rules are not counted towards United Kingdom qualifications or titles. All dogs must be registered with The Kennel Club but the dog need not be a pedigree and can be registered on the Obedience and Working Trials Register to ensure it complies with entry requirements.

Registration forms can be obtained from The Kennel Club, and a small fee is payable. No details of your dog's background need be given for the Obedience and Working Trials Register but, if you wish your dog to be registered under its breed, both parents must already be registered and other criteria must be met, such as obtaining the breeder's signature and proof of the dog's parentage. If your dog is a pedigree, the breeder may already have registered the litter, but you must make sure that you have transferred ownership into your own name, unless you are handling on the owner's behalf, or you will be in breach of KC Rules when you enter a trial. If your dog has not been registered previously and you do not intend to breed or show, it is probably easier to apply only for Obedience and Working Trials Registration.

There are WorkingTrial training societies in most parts of the country and a couple of national ones: the Associated Sheep, Police and Army Dog Society (ASPADS) and the British Association for German Shepherd Dogs (BAGSD). The Kennel Club will supply names of societies in your area, and most of them hold trials. Some also hold matches and rallies limited to members so, if you join your local society, you may get a chance to compete before entering a proper trial, and you will certainly get a lot of help and advice with your training.

One of the other advantages of getting together with other Working trial enthusiasts is that it is very hard to train alone. Eventually you will need help, if only to lay your track and set out your search square and, if you are very lucky, your club will have access to land for training (something often in short supply for Working Trials enthusiasts). When you are ready to start entering trials, the best means of keeping up with the news is to subscribe to *Working Trials Monthly*, the only magazine dedicated solely to trials and triallists, which is packed with information, trials dates, judge's reports and training tips. It is virtually impossible to keep in touch with the trials scene without this magazine.

(Opposite page) A typical entry form.

NAME OF SOCIETY

OPEN*/CHAMPIONSHIP* WORKING TRIALS

Venue*...
Dates*...
* Complete as per Schedule

Stake
Please use a separate entry form for each stake

CERTIFICATE OF ENTRY

Kennel Club requirements with regard to registration and transfer and where the Rules and Regulations can be obtained. Also information about qualification and the minimum age for entry.

Registered Name of Dog	Breed	Sex (D or B)	Breeder	Date of Birth	Sire	Dam

Qualified for entry at . . . . Open Trial on (Date must be stated) . . . .

Qualified for entry at . . . . Open Trial on (Date must be stated) . . . .

Qualified for entry at . . . . Championship Trial on . . . .

Qualified for entry at . . . . Championship Trial on . . . .

DECLARATION

Stating that you agree to be bound by Kennel Club Rules and Regulations and that your dog is eligible for entry and not liable to disqualification. You must also sign to say the dog is free from any contagious or infectious disease and is in good health and that, if the dog becomes infected or is in contact with any infectious or contagious disease within 21 days of the show, you will withdraw from competition.

USUAL SIGNATURE OF OWNER(S) . . . . DATE . . . .
NOTE: Dogs entered in breach of Kennel Club Regulations are liable to disqualification whether or not the owner was aware of the breach.

BLOCK LETTERS

NAME OF HANDLER . . . .

(Mr, Mrs or Miss) . . . .

ADDRESS . . . .

. . . .

TEL NO. . . . .

BLOCK LETTERS

NAME OF REGISTERED OWNER . . . .

(Mr, Mrs or Miss) . . . .

ADDRESS . . . .

. . . .

TEL NO. . . . .

All Working Trials, whether Open or Championship, are divided into stakes. Most societies schedule four stakes: Companion Dog (CD), Utility Dog UD), Working Dog (WD) and either Tracking Dog (TD) or Patrol Dog (PD). Where land is short, some societies may be forced to drop one of the tracking stakes, while those that are more fortunate with land will offer both TD and PD at the same trial. In general, however, trials tend to be either TD or PD.

When starting out most newcomers aim for the CD stake, although seasoned triallists who are bringing out a new dog will train for both CD and UD and enter either or both according to the status of the trial. As mentioned earlier, it is necessary to qualify in all stakes except CD at Open level before entering into Championship, so your first trial could be either a CD Championship or a UD Open, depending on how far you are prepared to travel and what is available to enter at the time.

The exercises are the same in Open and Championship trials but usually in Championship stakes the track is more intricate, the sendaway a little more challenging and the articles are smaller or more difficult. At an Open trial the Nosework and Control/Agility sections of the same stake are often judged by different judges, but at a Championship trial there is one judge for all groups of the stake. This means that competitors can complete in all groups of an Open stake in one day, although the trial may well run for several days. Handlers are given a choice of days to attend and, as far as possible, the Trials Manager will try to comply with their first choice.

At Championship trials the TD and PD Control and Agility and PD Patrol Groups are always on the last day of the trial and all Nosework is completed separately over the previous days. This is usually the case with the other stakes, although occasionally the lower stakes at Championship trials can be worked in one day with each judge judging Nosework for half a day and Control and Agility for the other half on each day of the trial. Championship trials can run over as much as eight days and opens usually last around three. This means that in Championship trials competitors are often called upon to complete their Nosework on a week-day and then return on the Sunday for the Control and Agility. For this reason, Working Trials are often seen as a pastime for the idle rich or retired. However, many working folk arrange their time off around trials, perhaps having several short breaks or odd days and turning their trials into holidays. This is especially so at the summer trials in Scotland and Scarborough, where many of the competitors stay for the whole week and enjoy the holiday atmosphere.

I shall describe individual exercises at a later stage but for now I shall just explain the stakes.

Companion Dog Stake (CD)

This is the only non-tracking stake, designed to introduce Working Trials to the new dog, or the new handler. As the name implies, a dog capable of qualifying at this level should be an obedient and well behaved companion.

Although the Control and Agility sections of this stake are quite demanding, Nosework is less of a challenge and most people who cross the obedience/Working Trial divide find this stake well within their capabilities. Open CD is for dogs who have not qualified CDEX or UDEX or won three or more first prizes in CD or any prize in a higher stake. At Championship level CD is open to dogs who have not won three or more first prizes in CD, more than one prize in UD or any prize in a higher stake. Exercises and total marks available are as follows:

Group 1 – Control

Heel on lead	5
Heel free	10
Recall to handler	5
Sendaway	10
Group Total	**30**
Minimum Qualifying Mark	**21**

Group 2 – Stays

Sit two minutes, handler out of sight	10
Down ten minutes, handler out of sight	10
Group Total	**20**
Minimum Qualifying Mark	**14**

Group 3 – Agility

Clear jump	5
Long jump	5
Scale (3), Wait (2), Return (5)	10
Group Total	**20**
Minimum Qualifying Mark	**14**

Group 4 – Retrieving and Nosework

Retrieve a dumbbell	10
Elementary search	20
Group Total	**30**
Minimum Qualifying Mark	**21**

Total Marks

Total marks available for CD stake	100
Minimum Qualification Marks:	
Open Certificate of Merit	80
Championship CD	70
Championship CDEX	80

Utility Dog (UD)

Many people believe this to be the first real trials stake as it includes both tracking and a full-size search square. At Open trials UD is for dogs who have not been awarded a Certificate of Merit in UD or in any higher stake and Championship is for dogs who have been awarded a CoM in Open UD but have not qualified Excellent in any higher stake. A dog cannot be entered in UD and WD at the same Championship trial.

Group 1 – Control

Heel free	5
Sendaway	10
Retrieve	5
Down stay ten minutes	10
Steadiness to gunshot	5
Group Total	**35**
Minimum Qualifying Mark	**25**

Group 2 – Agility

Clear jump	5
Long jump	5
Scale (3), Wait (2), Return (5)	10
Group Total	**20**
Minimum Qualifying Mark	**14**

Group 3 Nosework

Search	35
Track (90), Articles (10 +10 = 20)	110
Group Total	**145**
Minimum Qualifying Mark	**102**

Total Marks

Total marks available for UD stake 200
Minimum Qualification Marks:
Open Certificate of Merit 160
Championship UD 141
Championship UDEX 160

Working Dog (WD)

At this level dogs and handlers are expected to be a little more experienced, in that for Open stakes they must have been awarded a CoM in UD, although not in any higher stake, and for Championship trials they must have qualified UDEX and gained a CoM in Open WD.

Group 1 Control

Heel free 5
Sendaway 10
Retrieve 5
Down stay ten minutes 10
Steadiness to gunshot 5
Group Total **35**
Minimum Qualifying Mark **25**

Group 2 – Agility

Clear jump 5
Long Jump 5
Scale (3), Wait (2), Return (5) 10
Group Total: **20**
Minimum Qualifying Mark **14**

Group 3 – Nosework

Search 35
Track (90); Articles (10+10 = 20) 110
Group Total **145**
Minimum Qualifying Mark **102**

Total Marks

Total marks available for WD stake 200
Minimum Qualification Marks:
Open Certificate of Merit 160
Championship WD 141
Championship WDEX 160

Tracking Dog (TD)

By the time dog and handler reach this stake they will have gained considerable experience. At Open trials they must have been awarded a CoM in Open WD and for entry in Championship TD the dog must have qualified WDEX twice and gained two CoMs in Open TD.

Group 1 – Control

Heel free 5
Sendaway and redirect 10
Speak 5
Down stay ten minutes 10
Steadiness to gunshot 5
Group Total 35
Minimum Qualifying Mark 25

Group 2 – Agility

Clear jump 5
Long Jump 5
Scale (3), Wait (2), Return (5) 10
Group Total 20
Minimum Qualifying Mark 14

Group 3 – Nosework

Search 35
Track (100), Articles (10+10+10 = 30) 130
Group Total 165
Minimum Qualifying Mark 116

Total Marks

Total marks available for TD stake 220
Minimum Qualification Marks:
Open Certificate of Merit 176
Championship TD 155
Championship TDEX 176

Patrol Dog (PD)

Although this stake is at the same level as TD it has a whole new group of exercises and is designed for the handler and dog who want to try something different. It offers the chance to test the dog's courage and skill at finding, detaining and pursuing a criminal or criminals and the handler's absolute control in exciting and difficult situations. To enter this stake at

Open level the dog must have qualified WDEX and at Championship level it must have qualified WDEX twice as well as gaining a CoM in PD Open on two occasions.

Group 1 – Control

Heel free	5
Sendaway and redirect	10
Speak	5
Down stay ten minutes	10
Steadiness to gunshot	5
Group Total	**35**
Minimum Qualifying Mark	**25**

Group 2 – Agility

Clear jump	5
Long Jump	5
Scale (3), Wait (2), Return (5)	10
Group Total	**20**
Minimum Qualifying Mark	**14**

Group 3 – Nosework

Search	35
Track (60), Articles (10 +10 = 20)	80
Group Total	**115**
Minimum Qualifying Mark	**80**

Group 4 – Patrol

Quartering the ground	45
Test of courage	20
Search and sscort	25
Recall from criminal	30
Pursuit and detention of criminal	30
Group Total	**150**
Minimum Qualifying Mark	**105**

Total Marks

Total marks available for PD stake	320
Minimum Qualification Marks:	
Open Certificate of Merit	256
Championship PD	224
Championship PDEX	256

General Remarks

The stakes at Working Trials provide a steady route through to the top, allowing dog and handler to gain experience and reach a good standard in each stake before progressing to the next. Although the groups stay much the same throughout the stakes, the exercises within the groups become progressively more difficult, and this is reflected in the marks. New exercises are introduced in TD and a new group in PD, so training needs to be ongoing.

I am grateful to the *Kennel Club Year Book 1996/97* for verification of this information, but both stakes and qualifications are subject to alteration and, although correct at the time of writing, this information should be checked in the current Year Book's 'Rules and Regulations' section before you enter.

Heelwork

When I first became interested in Working Trials I had been competing in obedience competitions for many years and was a heelwork fanatic. I decided to go along to the only trial held in my area and see what it was all about. Not knowing any better I stationed myself near the Control and Agility area and proceeded to watch the competitors work the various exercises. As it was an Open trial one judge was judging the Control and Agility for all stakes, so it seemed to me that all the dogs were doing different exercises, with sendaways of various lengths and in different directions; and some dogs were asked to speak while others were not. As a graduate from the regimented world of obedience classes I found this all very strange. However, the heelwork was even stranger – all dogs worked at three different paces, but some were on the lead and some were not, and all seemed to work varying courses of different lengths!

I cringe now when I think how scathing I was of these dogs and their less-than-perfect heelwork. I made no allowances for the fact that some were raw beginners working at three different paces with no extra commands on rough ground and no ring ropes for guidance, and I made unfair comparisons between them and the near-perfect, dressage-like rounds I was used to seeing at obedience shows. Looking back, I realise that the fact that these same dogs had probably already completed a track and search square had escaped my notice, and anyway, as I had no idea

Heelwork: waiting to start.

Heelwork: slow pace.

Heelwork: normal pace.

Heelwork: fast pace.

Heelwork: about turn.

what that involved, I probably wouldn't have been impressed. Even the agility exercises left me cold; I dismissed them out of hand for their untidy heelwork. I look back now in horror and am ashamed of my initial impressions. Nevertheless, it is true to say that, in general, many trials dogs could improve their heelwork. However, once they are out of CD, this exercise only represents five marks and, with so many to train, this one takes a back seat. It is nevertheless worth remembering that, at ticket level, those five marks are precious, and even in the lower stakes a mark or two lost in heelwork can cost a qualifier. Trials heelwork is as good as the handler makes it and some trials dogs can, and do, hold their own in obedience competition. The best trials handlers train heelwork with the same dedication as their other exercises, and it shows.

In all stakes the heelwork is tested at normal, fast and slow pace, with no extra commands permitted. The dog's shoulder should stay reasonably close to the handler's leg through changes of direction, pace, and at the sit on halts. The judge may require the dog and handler to walk among or around people or obstacles or to perform a figure-of-eight, and the handler should walk in a smart, natural manner with the dog remaining at heel. It is worth noting that many trials judges penalise handlers for an 'unnatural' manner of walking, and the heelwork pose adopted by many obedience handlers, with their left hands held across their fronts or stationary against their legs, will often be seen as 'unnatural'. If in doubt, try walking at a brisk pace without your dog and see what your arms do – that is how the judge wants to see you walk with your dog.

Another point worth noting is that trials heelwork takes place on the Control field, which could be anything from grass to jungle. There are no ring ropes and the ground is often very wet or muddy and usually uneven, not to mention mole hills and cow pats, so precision heelwork is not just unwanted – it's impossible. I have heard of a judge who carried out a conversation with the handler during heelwork and expected replies, and another who set his heelwork course through a ditch and into a wood, so it is a mistake to think it is easy. What the judge is looking for is practical, attentive heelwork with the dog under control but relaxed and happy. You will not be marked for the dog going slightly wide or such things as crabbing (the dog moving with its body at an angle to the line of travel) but you will be penalised for the dog leaving your side, stopping, barking or refusing to sit. In general, if your dog is happy to be at your side at all paces (and in trials, *fast* means run!) and over any terrain, pays attention and sits smartly when you stop, you have practical trials heelwork. Anything more is up to you.

The Retrieve: throwing the dumbbell.

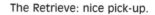

The Retrieve: nice pick-up.

The Retrieve: happy return.

The Retrieve: good present.

The Retrieve: finish to heel.

The Sendaway: setting up.

The Sendaway: sending.

The Sendaway: redirect.

The Recall

The recall to handler is only required in CD and is a very straightforward exercise. The handler will be directed to put the dog in either the sit or the down (handler's choice) and, on command from steward, leave the dog and walk a reasonable distance as directed, and then turn and face the dog. On steward's command the handler will call the dog, who should return smartly to the handler, sit in front and then finish to heel. The handler must wait for the steward's direction before commanding the dog. This exercise is worth five marks, and there is no reason why all five marks should not be gained.

The Retrieve

The dumbbell retrieve is included in CD, UD and WD stakes so it is worth getting it right from the start. The dog is required to wait at the handler's side while the dumbbell is thrown. Then, on steward's command, the handler will send the dog to fetch the dumbbell and return smartly to sit in front and present it. Once again, on steward's command, the handler will take the dumbbell and send the dog to heel. Because of the enthusiasm needed for nosework, trials handlers tend to encourage their dogs to pick up and carry anything from a very early age, so most dogs take readily to the dumbbell as just another article. However, in this exercise it might pay to take a leaf out of the obedience handler's book and teach the Retrieve a little more formally. The 'Hold it' command, taught early on by means of the dumbbell and away from nosework, can come in very useful later when an article in the search square lacks appeal. Once again, time taken in teaching this exercise well can result in five easy marks, or ten in CD.

The Sendaway

The sendaway exercise in any stake accounts for a great number of non-qualifiers. Some dogs appear to find this far more difficult than others, and some handlers have similar problems. Converts from obedience may lose their dog's enthusiasm for sendaway by insisting on the sort of accuracy required in a small ring, whereas in trials the ability to cover distance and take direction is more important.

In CD the minimum distance for a sendaway is 20yd (18m), and it is usually no more than about 30yd (27m), but in the higher stakes the minimum distance is 50yd (46m) and can be much further. For the first four stakes the handler will be asked to send the dog from a given point to a position indicated by the judge. Usually in CD this will be a barrier or obvious stopping point but, as the stakes progress, the destination may be less obvious. I have had such things as 'The bush in the hedge with berries on',

'The tall thistle in the distance', or even 'The right-hand back leg of that electricity pylon'. All this makes little difference to a dog who has been taught to run in a straight line to nothing until stopped, but those taught a send-to rather than a sendaway can end up very confused. In the lower stakes, when the dog has reached the designated area (or as near as the handler can get it) it must be stopped and kept still until the judge indicates his or her satisfaction. The dog should then be recalled, but the recall is not marked. Many handlers will drop the dog into a down when it reaches the desired spot, but this is not necessary as long as the dog remains stationary. In fact the down position can prove a disadvantage in TD and PD when the dog has to be redirected, because on uneven ground or in long grass you can't see the dog and the dog can't see you.

The Redirect

Any handler who has taught his or her dog to redirect early on will find it extremely useful in the lower stakes when the initial outrun has not gone according to plan. I learned this with my first trials dog, who was taught an obedience style sendaway and, once he stopped, nothing would move him other than a recall. A dog who will happily move around in any direction as indicated by its handler will keep scoring points but, if it is rooted to the spot and the spot in question is the wrong spot, there's little that you can do and there are no more marks to be had.

In TD and PD stakes

Speak on command.

the redirect (or directional control as it is correctly termed) is part of the sendaway and usually accounts for half the allotted marks. The handler will be asked to send the dog to a designated spot and stop it. When the judge has indicated his or her satisfaction with the dog's position the handler will be instructed to redirect the dog to another spot and stop it again once, or even twice. The judge will be looking for the dog that moves around happily and freely on instructions from its handler and, although extra commands will be noted, most judges will not mark too heavily if they consider the dog is responding well to the handler.

Steadiness to Gunshot

To the dog that is not noise shy these five marks are the easiest it will ever earn. However, for those that are sensitive it can be an absolute nightmare, and the anxiety caused by the anticipation of this test can upset other exercises. I was lucky in that my first trials dog appeared oblivious of gunshot to the extent that judges often asked me if he was deaf. This was not entirely luck as I had bred him myself and I make a point of banging tin trays, dropping tins of nails and generally making a hullabaloo when I have puppies, so mine are usually fairly bombproof. However, my next trials dog was a little bitch bred by someone who was obviously not as noisy as I am, and she was apprehensive of the gun. We got over this, and she's fine now, but it made me aware of how important this exercise is.

There is no gun test in CD and, although part of the Control group of exercises in the other stakes, it is usually carried out on the tracking field. This is to prevent interference with any other dog, as only one dog is present on the tracking field at any one time. The test will not be incorporated into any other exercise and the competitor will always be told when the gun is to be fired. The judge may require the dog to be walking to heel or to be away from the handler but, however it is carried out, the handler must be within controlling distance of the dog. The judge will penalise any dog that barks or shows fear or aggression. For the dog who is upset by the gun the whole tracking field can become a place of fear, and this can be reflected in its nosework if it is anticipating the gun at the end, so it pays to take time to teach this exercise and be patient. It is better to wait until the dog is rock steady than to enter it too soon and risk spoiling the other exercises.

Speak on Command

This is another test of the dog's character, for some dogs love their voices, while others will not 'speak'. Although not introduced until TD and PD level, speaking should be encouraged from day one. If the dog has spent its trials career in silence it will be amazed by a handler who suddenly wants it, as a mature dog, to speak. However, most puppies will yap with the right sort of encouragement and, if this can be worked on, it can result in a reliable speak. In TD and PD stakes the judge may think up some weird and wonderful situations for the dog to speak. The judge may ask the handler to get the dog to speak while walking at heel, but can also direct the handler to leave the dog in a given position and carry out various instructions whilst commanding the dog to speak. I have heard of handlers instructed to sit on a chair, climb up a step ladder, walk round a search square collecting the poles or even walk circles around the jumps whilst asking their dogs to speak and cease speaking as directed. The judge will be looking for the dog who responds immediately to commands to speak and cease speaking and will penalise a dog for not starting, stopping or maintaining the speak. So once you have your dog speaking it is a good idea to think of as many strange situations and locations for practice as possible so that nothing comes as a surprise.

Stays

Other than in the CD stake, where there is a two-minute sit which, if practical, will be out of sight, stays remain the same throughout all the stakes: 10 minutes down out of sight. In the sit and the down, dogs can be tested on their own or as part of a group. In all stakes, the 10-minute down stay is often carried out in two groups, but I have seen the CD sit stay done individually after the search and retrieve. It makes little difference where or when the dog is asked to stay as this is about control and, if it is properly taught, 'stay' means 'stay'. Once again, these are easy marks; the dog doesn't have to do anything, but any movement can result in all marks being lost, so the wise handler is thorough in training this exercise. Stay, like speak, is about confidence and, again, it pays to practise this exercise in unusual surroundings with unexpected distractions. The confident, relaxed dog will stay happily where you leave it, secure in the belief that you will return.

When you tell people that you compete in Working Trials they do not usually ask about the track or control: a look of horror comes over their faces and they tell you they could never ask their dog to do the scale! I can understand this fear as the scale does look quite formidable. Nevertheless, it is often the people rather than the dogs who have a problem with this; most dogs, if they are fit, appear to have little difficulty with this obstacle. The Agility group consists of three elements and, in CD and UD, all jumps are reduced for the smaller dogs. This group remains unchanged for the larger dogs throughout the stakes and beyond UD the jumps are no longer reduced. The test consists of just three elements and I will deal with each one separately.

The Clear Jump.

The Long Jump.

The Clear Jump

Construction

This jump must be a minimum of 3ft (0.9m) wide, upright in construction and in no way injurious to the dog. The top rail, which should be rigid, will be set at the required height and the space below may be left open or filled in, although any infilling must not go above the bottom of the top rail. It should be easy to see whether the dog touches the top rail and casual fouling will be penalised. Excessive pressure on the bar or knocking it down will result in a failure. The height of the clear jump varies with the size of dog in the lower two stakes but remains at 3ft throughout all stakes for dogs over 15in (38cm) at the shoulder. In CD and UD, dogs up to10in (25cm) at the shoulder will need to clear 1ft 6in (0.5m) and for dogs over 10in and up to 15in the height is 2ft (0.6m), but there is no provision for smaller dogs in the higher stakes.

Procedure

The clear jump is always the first of the three elements and can be followed by the long jump or the scale. The approach to the clear jump is very much the handler's choice; it makes no difference to the marks whether handler and dog approach together or the dog is sent ahead or called up. However, the handler must at no time touch or walk beyond any part of the jump before the dog has jumped. The handler will be told from which side to approach the jump and will then be allowed to command the dog to jump in its own time. Having negotiated the jump, the dog must remain on the other side until joined by the handler on steward's command, and will be penalised heavily for returning past the jump.

The Scale: over.

The Scale: wait.

The Scale: return.

The Long Jump

Construction

The long jumps consists of five elements, although in the lower stakes the smaller dogs have just four. Each individual element slopes from front to back and increases in height, from the first, which is 4in (10cm) at the front and 7in (18cm) at the back, to the fifth, which is 8in (20cm) at the front to 11in (28cm) at the back. The top of each element must be at least 6in (15cm) wide and the width of each element is graduated from front to back, the first being no less than 3ft (0.9m) and the fifth no less than 3ft 8in (1.1m). When set out, the five elements should span a distance of 9ft (8.3m) for all stakes other than CD and UD. In these, for small dogs entered, the distance shall be 4ft (1.2m) for dogs up to 10in (25cm) at the shoulder and 6ft (1.8m) for dogs over 10in and up to 15in (38cm).

Procedure

Once again, how to approach this jump is the handler's choice. Most handlers like to pace out the distance for take-off and tend to leave the dog and walk a set number of paces before setting up the dog to jump. However, there are several variations. The handler must not go beyond the first element of the long jump until after the dog has jumped. He or she will then be instructed to join the dog, who must remain at the other end of the jump until released by the handler on steward's command. Any contact with the jump will be marked, and the dog will be heavily penalised for jumping out to the side or coming back beyond the end of the jump before being released.

The Scale

Construction

The scale is a wooden structure made up of planks, which form a vertical wall. It may have a slightly padded top and three slats on either side of the top half, and is usually secured to prevent movement. The height for all stakes is 6ft (1.8m), but it is lowered for the smaller dogs in CD and UD to a height of 3ft (0.9m) for dogs up to 10in (25cm) and 4ft (1.2m) for dogs over 10in and up to 15in (38cm).

Procedure

The scale must be approached from the side indicated by the steward. Handler and dog should walk together and halt within 9ft (2.7m) of the scale. This distance will be marked for the handler's benefit. Then, in the handler's own time, the dog should be ordered to scale. On landing, the dog will be commanded by the handler to take up a pre-nominated position (stand, sit or down) and then, on steward's command, the handler will recall the dog over the scale. Dogs will be penalised for failure to scale, failure to take up the right position or to wait and failure to recall.

General Remarks

Dogs who fail or refuse any of the jumps may be allowed a second attempt for half marks at the judge's discretion, depending on the stake.

All these jumps, at the right height for the size of dog, are within the capabilities of any fit, reasonably agile dog. Problems are more likely to be with attitude to jumping than with ability and any lack of confidence in the handler is usually conveyed to the dog. If you doubt this, take your dog out and ask it to jump natural obstacles. I think you will find that, however high the fence or wide the ditch, your dog will manage it as part of a relaxed walk.

Dogs and equipment ready for action!

Most triallists consider Nosework to be the most important aspect of Working Trials and it is true that at Championship trials, where Nosework takes place on a separate day, if the dog fails to qualify in this section there is no point in coming back for the rest, no matter how good it may be. As the stakes get higher the Nosework becomes more challenging and at the highest level the Tracking Dog title signifies the importance of the Nosework. Strangely enough, although competitors recognise the difficulty and the importance of this group of exercises, most of them do not worry about it while getting terribly strung up about the Control and Agility. One competitor summed this up when he said that, whereas Control relied heavily on his ability as a trainer and a handler, Nosework was down to the dog. This is ultimately true, for we cannot know where the track goes or the articles are placed; however, the right motivation and guidance at the outset can result in a confident and careful tracking dog, and good handling on the tracking field can assist an inexperienced youngster. This is apparent when we see the same handlers bringing out new dogs and achieving good Nosework marks right from the start. However, they must still have dogs with ability, for although it is possible for a really competent Nosework dog to carry a less able handler, even a top class handler cannot make a dog track!

When I first became interested in Working Trials I talked with a police dog handler, who told me that there was no better feeling than getting up early on a misty morning, just as the sun was rising, and following your dog round a track. As a person who was more used to going out in brilliant sunshine in the middle of the day and working my dog around cut grass obedience rings, I couldn't see the attraction and didn't think I ever would, but now I know what he meant, and he was right. The adrenaline buzz that comes from knowing your dog is following a trail that is completely hidden to you is exhilarating, especially when your dog proves it by dropping on to an almost invisible article. No matter how many times it happens, it never ceases to thrill. Failures are disappointing, but make success that much more rewarding.

Search Squares

In CD stake there is no tracking and the only Nosework test is an elementary search, but in all other stakes the search usually follows the track, although sometimes a judge will do it the other way round. A search square is an area

Search Squares: setting up.

Search Squares: locating an article.

Search Squares: returning.

Search Squares: play and praise.

of ground marked out by four corner posts. It must be fresh for each dog, and must not be used again until the following day. The steward will place a number of articles within the marked area as directed by the judge, and the dog must find two to qualify. New but identical articles will be used for each dog, and they should be of a size and type that is suitable for the

Tracking: leaving the pole.

nature of the land and the level of the stake. In CD the area is 15yd (4.6m) square and there are three articles to find in four minutes, but in all the other stakes the area is 25yd (7.6m) square, with four articles to find in five minutes. The handler should position himself on one side of the square (having regard to wind direction) and send the dog in to search. Verbal encouragement and movement around the square is permitted but the handler must not enter the square and the dog must locate and return the articles to hand to score maximum marks.

The marks are usually divided so that a percentage is allotted to each article and a percentage to style, so the dog who carries out the search in a business-like manner and retrieves all articles may score maximum marks but a dog who locates all articles by luck or is messy in the pick-up, slow on the return or mouths or drops the articles will lose marks. An enthusiastic dog who enjoys the search and wants its handler to share its 'find' can often locate even the most difficult articles and score valuable marks. Time spent from a very early age in teaching a tiny puppy the fun and joy of articles is

Tracking: on track.

time well spent, and an almost obsessive desire for anything from a small piece of carpet to a cartridge case can pay off, both in the square and on the track. Once you become hooked on working trials you will find yourself turning into a magpie and collecting anything and everything that might be seen as an article. I have been caught swooping in on discarded pieces of Venetian blinds, till roll middles and corks from wine bottles. My non-doggy friends think me very sad, but I had the last laugh when the thief who broke into my car to steal what looked like a bag of goodies ended up with toilet roll middles, old rags, pieces of hose-pipe and squares of carpet – I would love to have seen his face!

Tracking

To me, tracking will always be the biggest mystery in trials. It took me ages even to begin to get the hang of handling a dog on the end of the tracking line and if, as a wise triallist once told me, failure is a learning experience, I must be one of the most learned handlers around. In the CD stake there is no tracking, but all the other stakes have tracks varying in age and complexity according to the level of the stake. For each dog competing, a track-layer walks a track. This could be over any type of terrain, from grass to growing crops or rolled plough. A marker will be placed at the beginning of the track and, for the UD stake, a second marker will indicate the direction of the track. In all other stakes, once the initial marker pole has been placed the track-layer will walk off in a direction and pattern predetermined by the judge and lay articles supplied by the judge (identical for each dog) along the track. Each dog in the stake will have a separate track on fresh ground, which cannot be used again until the following day. Straight stretches are referred to as legs, and the number of legs, turns and articles on each track is determined by the level of the stake. Once walked, the track will be allowed to age and, once again, the length of time it is left depends on what stake is being worked. A UD track must be at least 30 minutes old and have two articles, one of which should be laid in the first half of the track, and a minimum of one must be recovered to qualify. The WD will be at least one-and-a-half hours old with two articles, at least one of which must be recovered to qualify. In PD the track is two hours old, and again there are two articles, one needed to qualify. In TD the track is three hours old and three articles have been placed, at least two of which must be retrieved to qualify. In all stakes one of the articles will mark the end of the track.

Tracking: tracking powerfully on stubble.

When the dog is brought on to the tracking field the judge will take the competitor's number and indicate both the start pole and the direction in which the track-layer walked into the track. The handler will then prepare the dog, which should be tracked on a harness and line. The harness allows the dog to indicate the track by pulling and can be of leather or webbing with a top ring for the line. The line can be leather, rope or webbing according to the handler's preference, and is usually around 30ft (9m) in length and should be attached to the harness on the top ring so that it does not pass under the dog. When the dog is harnessed and ready the handler should indicate the start of the track to the dog, who should then pick up the direction of the first leg and start tracking. The track-layer will stand with the judge throughout the track and report on the dog's accuracy, and the judge will be looking for the dog to track straight lines with good concentration and commitment and without unnecessary casting or deviation, locating and indicating articles along the track by stopping, returning to the handler or lying down. Marks will be lost for untidy tracking or breaks in concentration, and marks will be gained for every article found. Judges mark according to their ideal and track marks are often as much to do with style as actual faults. If the dog loses the track and does not recover, or if it makes a mistake and goes off in the wrong direction, the competitor will either be called or whistled off to prevent fouling an adjacent track.

No matter how good dogs and handlers are, they will sometimes fail tracks. Many things can have an effect on tracking conditions and what one dog may find easy another will struggle with. Weather conditions and terrain play a part and strong wind can make a track virtually impossible to follow, whilst dry rolled plough with no growth is almost equivalent to a hard-surface track. Wise handlers teach their dogs well and then accept what they get – at the end of the day, we cannot follow the track, so how can we presume to know better?

PATROL

Working trials do not really constitute a spectator sport. Tracks in far distant fields do not often draw an audience and even Control is sometimes too far away from the gate to be watched easily. Patrol work is a different matter. It is usually the last group to be judged, and is often still going on when the other stakes are finished, so competitors gather in anticipation of some good entertainment. As far as possible, Trials Managers tend to put the Patrol group in an easily accessible location, knowing the interest, and judges try to make their test as entertaining as possible for the onlookers. Traditionally, this stake has less competitors than TD, possibly because of the tremendous time and dedication needed to teach a whole new series of exercises as well as keeping all the others up to scratch. The PD stake is at the same level as TD, so dogs entered have already reached a high level of control and obedience. As the Patrol round is based on man-work, absolute control is essential and the recall from a running 'criminal', which is always part of the PD round, demonstrates the implicit obedience of these highly motivated dogs.

Dog locates 'criminal' and 'speaks'.

The five Patrol exercises are always the same, although judges may put their own interpretation on the scene setting.

Quartering the Ground

The first test is Quartering the Ground, which is essentially a search and locate exercise in which the dog is sent to find a person hidden somewhere on the patrol field, out of sight of dog and handler. Once it has located the person, the dog should signal its find and 'hold' the person by spontaneously barking, continuing to bark until joined by its handler. The dog may be tested by the offer of food during this exercise, both by hand and thrown on the ground, and will be penalised for eating the food, leaving the area, or failing to bark or to maintain barking.

Test of Courage

Next comes the Test of Courage, and this may take just about any form, as it is very much left to the judge's discretion. I have seen many variations of this exercise; the dogs have had to face buckets of water being thrown, huge leafy branches and bin bags being waved, dustbin lids being banged, shouting, car horns or even gun fire, and whatever the threat the dog must show no fear and be prepared to challenge the aggressor. In this test the dog is expected to work on its own initiative; handler control is not required.

Search and Escort

The Search and Escort test requires the dog to be positioned so that it can watch and guard the 'criminal' whilst the handler carries out a search and then, together with the handler, escort the 'criminal' as directed by the judge. During this escort, the 'criminal' will make an attempt to attack the handler, who should be defended by the dog. The dog should cease the attack either on command from its handler or when the 'criminal' stands still, and the initial attack may be spontaneous or on the handler's command. The judge will be looking for instant response from the dog and the strategic positioning of the dog by the handler, and may ask questions on this.

Recall from Criminal

One of the most difficult of the tests is the Recall from Criminal and, with 30 marks to be gained, it pays to get it right. The handler will be approached by a 'criminal' who, after a brief but unheated exchange of words, will run away. The dog, who is off the lead and at heel at this time, will be sent on

Dog watches 'criminal' to prevent escape.

judge's instruction to handler to chase the fleeing man but, when approximately half way between handler and 'criminal', it will be recalled by verbal command or whistle and should cease the chase and return to the handler. If the dog fails to respond the 'criminal' will continue to run to indicate that the dog is still chasing. The handler may be penalised for using too many commands but, if the dog fails to 'call off' or shows a lack of commitment in the initial chase, no marks are gained.

Pursuit and Detention of Criminals

The final and possibly most exciting part of PD is the Pursuit and Detention of Criminals. Once again, this test is staged according to the judge's own interpretation and is usually part of an entertaining scenario with amusing verbal exchanges for the benefit of the onlookers. The test calls for the handler to engage the 'criminal' in conversation and, after an exchange of words, the dog will be sent to pursue the fleeing man and bring him to a halt. The dog may do this by taking hold of the protected arm of the man and hanging on, by knocking him down or by preventing his movement by circling. This test may include more than one 'criminal' and the dog will have to chase and detain as directed by his handler. If the dog is unable to prevent the criminal's escape it can be seen as a lack of commitment and, as well as not gaining marks in this test, the dog will not be tested at the Recall from Criminal exercise or, if the test has already taken place, will lose any marks gained on that test.

General Remarks

Unfortunately, there is some controversy about the PD stake, with some people thinking it encourages aggression and should not be part of trials. I can only assure them by saying that, of all the great PD dogs I have met, I have never known one that was anything but friendly. This test is about finding, chasing and holding the 'toy' which, for PD, is the padded sleeve worn by the criminal. The reward is to win the sleeve, and the joy comes from the instinct to hunt and capture prey, which is common to all dogs.

Dog prevents 'criminal' from escaping.

Game over, dog receives his 'toy' – the padded sleeve.

The man is the means to an end, and I have never seen a PD dog who was not happy to greet the 'criminal' as a friend at the end of a test. Any tendency to a macho image in handlers is soon overcome by the need for implicit control. There is no place for aggression in dogs or handlers in the Patrol Dog stake. To prove my point, one of the greatest PD dogs I have known, who won both civilian and police dog trials, was a Border Collie called Angus who was also a registered PAT (Pets As Therapy) dog.

YOUR FIRST TRIAL

Sooner or later you will be ready to enter a trial, and this is usually, but not always, prompted by one being in your area, perhaps even organised by your own society. Entries are made on entry forms which come inside the trial schedule. Make sure you send for a schedule in good time as entries usually close a month to six weeks before the trial. The entry forms are self-explanatory and should be filled in according to the information already supplied to The Kennel Club when you registered your dog. You have to sign to say that the dog is in good health and that you agree to abide by KC Rules, and it is up to you to withdraw your dog if its state of health deteriorates before the date of the trial. When you send off your entry form and fee, a stamped self-addressed envelope should be enclosed to allow the Trials Manager to inform you of the day and time to report. If for any reason you need to withdraw from competition it is very important to let the

Working trials do not normally boast organised sites, like obedience competitions –
a barn in a rural location is a typical trials base.

organiser know, to prevent needless waste of time and land by walking tracks that are not required.

Once your entry has been accepted you will be sent your report time, and most societies send clear maps showing how to reach the base. Do not forget this, as most trials bases are not easy to find and can be anything from a farm-yard to a lay-by.

When you set off for the trial, make sure that you have the essentials – dog, collar and lead, dumbbell, harness and line, wellies, waterproofs, and water for the dog. Anything over and above this is non-essential and it won't be a disaster if you forget. Most venues have some sort of refreshments on offer and many societies are renowned for the quality of their catering, especially the bacon butties. Don't rely on this, though – some don't even have coffee!

When you arrive at the trial, report first to the base steward, who will be able to give you all the information you need. He or she will tell you where you can exercise your dog, where your Control field is and the Stay times. Stays may be done at the base or on the Control field and you should make sure you know where they are to be. If your track time is already decided the steward will tell you the time and when and where to report and if you will need an escort. Because of the area needed to run a trial it is often necessary for competitors to be escorted to their tracking field as they may never find it. If this is the case the base steward will tell you when and where to report to meet your escort, who will then drive to your tracking field so that you can follow. Sometimes a draw is made between several competitors to determine tracking times and, if this is the case, it will be done at the base at your report time, so it is important not to be late.

At Championship trials, Nosework is always done first and may be all you do on that day so, once you have completed all your Nosework, you are free to leave. If you are not on qualifying marks and therefore not returning for the Control it is polite to inform the base steward and withdraw. At Open trials you will be expected to fit in your Control and Agility around your Nosework so, once you know your track time, you must decide whether to work your Control and Agility before or after the Nosework.

The order of work for the Control and Agility is usually determined either by queuing or putting your number down on a list and working to that order. It is as well to familiarise yourself with the location and layout of the Control field when you arrive so you are not left searching for it two minutes before the Stays.

Trials are very informal and, once you have established your timing, exercised your dog and located your work areas you are free to come and go as you please. Many competitors go and watch other stakes in progress and some like to watch the higher stakes track. If you decide you would like to do this, please make sure you ask both the competitor and the judge if they mind you watching. Needless to say, you cannot watch the tracks for your own stake until after you have worked.

When you have completed the Nosework, whatever the outcome, remember to thank the judge, track-layer and square steward. They do not get paid for their services and many are giving up their holidays or time off to make it possible for you to work your dog. The same applies to your Control judge and steward – a word of thanks is always much appreciated. If you have managed to qualify at the end of all the groups you will be awarded a certificate at the end of the day, signed by the judge, which will mean more to you than any prize or rosette. However, if you are awarded a place or even a win, this will not be presented until the end of the trial. If you are not there on that day it will need to be collected or sent on to you.

You will find after a while that most trials folk are very friendly and you will soon begin to know faces and make friends. Because of the lack of competitiveness in the lower stakes handlers are most appreciative of each other's efforts and sympathetic to failure – they have all been there. Do remember that the trials world is very small and whatever you can do to help with your society or with a trial will be very valuable. Without adequate help, trials cannot run, so enjoy your trialling, be successful but remember to do your bit.

I do hope this book will inspire some of you to have a go at trialling and others to understand that it is a bit more than dogs doing poor heelwork. For me, there is no better hobby, and I think my dogs would agree. Happy trialling!

The Kennel Club

The Kennel Club
1-5 Clarges Street
Piccadilly
London
W1Y 8AB

The Scottish Kennel Club

The Scottish Kennel CLub
8 Brunswick Place
Edinburgh
EH7 5HP

The Irish Kennel Club Ltd

The Irish Kennel Club Ltd
Fottrell House
Unit 36
Greenmount Office Park
Dublin 6 W
Republic of Ireland

Working Trials Monthly

Working Trials Monthly
WTM Publishing
Greenacres
Brades Road
Prees
Whitchurch
Shropshire
SY13 3DX

ASPADS

ASPADS
Membership Secretary:
Mr A T Bowles
Cobwebs
School Lane
Chearsley
Bucks
HP18 OBT

BAGSD

BAGSD
Secretary: Ms A Tohme
5 Westbrook Court
Westbrook Vale
Evercreech
Shepton Mallet
Somerset
BA4 6JN